we live
in the newn
of small difl

we live
in the newness
of small differences

EYEWEAR PUBLISHING

SOHINI BASAK

**WINNER OF THE INTERNATIONAL BEVERLY PRIZE FOR LITERATURE 2017
JUDGED BY KELLY DAVIO**

First published in 2018
by Eyewear Publishing Ltd
Suite 333, 19-21 Crawford Street
Marylebone, London W1H 1PJ
United Kingdom

Cover design and typeset by Edwin Smet
Printed in England by TJ International Ltd, Padstow, Cornwall

All rights reserved
© 2018 Sohini Basak

The right of Sohini Basak to be identified as author of
this work has been asserted in accordance with section 77
of the Copyright, Designs and Patents Act 1988

ISBN 978-1-912477-11-1

WWW.EYEWEARPUBLISHING.COM

for
Dipti Biswas *and* Bani Biswas

Sohini Basak

grew up in Barrackpore, India.
She studied literature and creative writing at
the universities of Delhi, Warwick, and East
Anglia, where she was awarded the Malcolm
Bradbury Continuation Grant for Poetry.
Currently, she lives in Delhi, making up
stories set around a hospital
for plants.

TABLE OF CONTENTS

AN ENCLOSURE – 9
PLOT – 10
SORTING WINTER DAYS – 11
THE BRIGHTEST THING I SAW TODAY WAS A DEAD KINGFISHER ON THE ROAD – 12
LIGHTNING NEVER STRIKES IN STRAIGHT LINES – 17
WHAT WILL BE GLASS – 18
WHAT I CAN'T DISTIL – 19
THEY HAVE MORE TO SAY – 20
CARRYING AROUND MY ANGER – 21
OTHER SMALL DISASTERS – 22
SUCK MARROW FROM SPINE – 23
MNEMONIC – 24
IF YOU LOOK LONG ENOUGH – 25
HOW TO BREED LILACS – 26
YOUR SUCCULENTS NEED A DROUGHT – 27
DIM LIGHT – 29
PICKLING – 30
PORAGHATI – 31
I LOST TIME SITTING OPPOSITE YOU IN THE LIBRARY – 33
WHY DID YOU STOP WRITING – 34
FUTURE LIBRARY: SOME ANXIETIES – 36
SALT – 37
LIKENESS – 38
HAZARDOUS – 41
DREAM ARGUMENT – 42
NORTH DELHI, WINTER – 43
SETTING – 44
TRAINING MY EAR: A JOURNAL – 45
PAPER SONG – 46
BY A DIFFERENT LINE – 47
HARE'S BREATH – 48
FUTURE LIBRARY: A FOOTNOTE – 49
IS IT COLD OR AM I TIRED OF THE DUST – 51
POSSIBLY OCTAGONAL – 52

IT IS COLD, AND I AM TIRED OF THE DUST – 53
AT 2 A.M., I CONFLATED EVERYONE AND EVERYTHING – 54
FUTURE LIBRARY: ALTERNATIVE ENDING – 56
15 AUGUST 2017 – 57
DINOSAUR ON WHEELS – 58
CORRESPONDENCE – 63
ERRATA – 65

AND OTHER STORIES

[WHEN A BIRD] – 68
BABUI – 69
TUNTUNI – 70
CHORUI – 71
KAAK – 72
CHEEL – 73
[THERE WAS NOTHING] – 74
BABUI – 75
[THE BIRD SAVED] – 76
[A QUESTION] – 78
HARICHACHA – 79
[THE FIRST THING] – 80
BOK – 81
SHOKUN – 82
[ANOTHER QUESTION] – 83
[THEN NOTHING] – 84
GUBGUBI PAKHI – 86
MURGI – 87
[THE ROOM IS FULL] – 88
[SOME FACTS] – 89
PYANCHA – 90
[WHEN A BIRD] – 92

NOTES – 94
ACKNOWLEDGEMENTS – 96

AN ENCLOSURE

not in language, but something more
private, hence inseparable, like a birthmark
on the thigh, this need to eat, to chew
before swallowing – what does not happen
to me happens elsewhere after all.

I was not always here, I am often not
present. In my dream, for example,
a dank yellow sky pinks up in patches,
hangs unkindly over our little town
flooded, the electricity wires snap and I
am hauling two large suitcases on ropes
to a rooftop with my brother –

between the effort of it and the waking
are a few minutes of sleep paralysis where
someone not in the room tells me you
are not going to be able to see the world
any more, you have no will to live.

Next to my bed, a jar with water, stale
from stems, and a line drops into my head
which I save for later. Sick with feeling
feelings of an imminent loss, the news
is pushed in to my room like a mass
of small animals, bleached coral dead.

What we cannot measure, we are
happy to let go, what does not happen
to us, we are likely to forget –

there is a pettiness in clocks, admit it now:
you love all your things. Illicit the lilies lie;
they want to know: what is time to trees?

PLOT

A mongoose evaluates the afternoon
backyard, its soil kiln-dry, sprouting
discarded pipes, batteries, an upturned
commode, but under the guava tree, she digs
up the ghosts of flowers with her charcoal
feet, renames each weed, each unloved root
with her nose, even as her pampas grass tail
consoles the hibiscus birthless this winter;
then, hitting the boundary wall, she decides
to make a tunnel connecting this once garden
to the world of water buffaloes, cranes – no
movement escapes these agate eyes, while dusk
falls the sky thickens to help the krait slink away
and here is when, if we blink, we lose the plot.

SORTING WINTER DAYS

seeing four new buildings surrounding our house each day
shadowing our rooms, my mother sighs, says how much more
sensible it would have been if our terrace were built facing
south, instead of facing the opposite side as it always has done
since our house was built twelve years ago. she sighs again,
says, i should have been an architect. but instead she is a doctor,
she switched from drawing lines to cells. the rain-lily bed, she says,

would have got the best of winter sunlight had it faced the other way.
who knew of those blueprints then? so we alter our rooms instead,
we bring the dining table upstairs, chipping bits of the stairwell wall
while hauling its glass top. we turn the living room into a bedroom,
wake up to a new set of curtains and pretend our world has turned around.
wherever we can, we shuffle picture frames, rearrange books on each shelf,
weigh out old spaces dreading squares of washed out walls, we exchange

door knobs, we move what we can since we cannot, or, we
dare not change our lives entirely, we live in the newness of small
differences, we crowd old pillowcases with embroidery so our
dreams enter our sleep again, we turn the soil in the rain-lily bed, its
deeper earth we bring to the surface, we sit outside late into the afternoon
doing little much. i count off stars as they first appear, while my mother
draws, her finger on the sky, an even cityscape that shifts as a cloud.

THE BRIGHTEST THING I SAW TODAY WAS A DEAD KINGFISHER ON THE ROAD
OR
WHAT I REALLY WANT TO TELL YOU

i.
we had to see the blue pines
to believe their blueness

we had seen prayer flags
tied between one mountain top
and another, a ravine in between,
but could not believe no engines
were involved

during that five-hour hike, our city lungs
contracted after every ten steps

the higher we climbed, the more purple
wild flowers became, then a voice said:
bless the trees that let you use their ancient
roots as ladder rungs

bless the mountains that don't grow back

after seven hundred more steps, we reached
Tiger's Nest and Phung-Su finally told us
what we were there to hear him say:

you do not come to pray for yourself here
someone else is praying for you,
so you pray for someone else

the sparrows in those hills had heads of gold

ii.

in a dream, i opened the refrigerator door
and forty tiger cubs rolled out
onto the floor, ice stuck to their damp bodies
which were neither soft nor hard from dying
in my dream, i set fire to the rug –

outside the dream, under the chandelier, i cried,
the table was full: china, soup spoons and an excess
of silverware that rang out over and over again:
your hands are more solid if you are raised an atheist

your hands have more blood –
i want you to think about this, even believe
me when i say: there cannot be any god,
at least not one with hands
or fully-formed eyes

between the door and this world
another world empties out
all its seeds in some dark water,
breathes in, but can barely breathe out
everything there has taken to eating dirt

iii.

terrifying the number of aeroplanes

i want to say i love animals,
so i cannot believe in god,
i want love, want animals,
so i cannot trust this is-or-is-not
    thing
    called god

by the riverbank, the body of a water buffalo
with bulging belly and bulging eye
comic in death

our desire to be always right
floated up like a claustrophobe's
polythene head

i want to say i love you,
but the riverside's choked up –
so terrifying the number of lungs
that need to breathe

as long as you live, nothing
ever stops: belief, disbelief, is the moment still asking?

iv.

instead, i tell you the story of November:
five o'clock in another country, again,
first steps into the late woods
an unanticipated quickness of fog
over a field that stretched out and touched
the cheek of a sudden rising moon

wasn't there then something absolutely black
wasn't it a shaking of a wild head on a neck
something across the branches and then
the longest minute of stillness, an acute
awareness of gravel and fear of an animal
who was the only other animal breathing
in that landscape, with a strong jaw –

this memory about the non-wolf: false
false animal in the wrong country
or wrong country around true animal
a study in eeriness like now, studies
of reindeer corpses locked in permafrost

a waking fever dream blazing like wild fire
the woods thick and real like a fox's red fur
and one by one – all memory, no animal

v.
unable to remember the turn to take
we stop to ask for directions –
on the traffic island, a pig with sewage
on her feet, some on her back,
her eyes closed as she tears at grass,
her tiny children suck at her from below

if it weren't for the animals, wouldn't every street
in this town look the same? unable to remember
the order of the words i meant to say them in –

when i say bless, i really mean conserve,
       help grow, love in the little ways you can
when i say bless, when i say a prayer,
       i really hope you don't hate
       or harm what lets you breathe

what should i stand next to so that you
see how small i am how insignificant

you hold my hand in the taxi and i marvel
at the streetlights being there in the same city
as us, but later, you tell me it's nothing, just
the way anything encounters anything else:
somewhat human somewhat algorithm

my sadness festers into an anger then fizzles out
like any other feeling i have for you –

but some sights i want to show you: a white
donkey luminous by the roadside in the hills
at four a.m. as our car goes past it

perhaps everything will light up like that in posterity

LIGHTNING NEVER STRIKES IN STRAIGHT LINES

You learn the redundancy of flowerpots barefoot
on a rooftop, after a storm, standing amongst
greener leaves and bleeding terracotta.

However, the way to view spilt milk with dry eyes
is to see the spillover as clouds on the floor,
to let a cat in and watch her lap up the sky.

To live through such sandpaper days, you must savour
the rough edges and unmake the bed until you find
last year's beliefs lying fabric still amongst its creases.

WHAT WILL BE GLASS

We had not fallen asleep, but had we woken up before?
A room so incorrigibly bright that all walls were windows.
Someone laughing outside, neck-deep in winter grass: you
thought that last night's brain fever sailed in right through
with that laughter. Well, my version is more fiction, less fog.
Or the comfort in darkness. Were we counting clouds, or the
number of evening walkers looking up at clouds? Nothing
beyond our fingers, in any case. Over fields, white bodies of
birds puncturing a less-white sky. A deer, or as usual, endless
dog bark. April's slow hours stretched out and wrapped around
a sapling's thin arms. If we are lucky: we will never remember
the same details. A strange belonging – or some strange light.

WHAT I CAN'T DISTIL

Years I shared a soul with a black and white cat. Years objects
spoke to us. Nights that refused to go because I could not sleep.

Mornings resembling miracles just for arriving. How food became
paper on chewing. The year leaves kept me company. A summer

of only wanting to hear Japanese being spoken, being sung. Finding
Szymborska. Never seeing grandmother angry. Learning about water

hyacinths. The colour violet. The colour blue. The amount of light
that makes all the difference between the colours violet and blue.

Carrying house keys to school and feeling important. The world seen
through brother's stamp collection. Or a hand-me-down school atlas.

Plants in early morning light. Watering plants one early morning. Watering
light. Not wanting to become a doctor. Being perpetually afraid of touching

a butterfly thinking one of us would explode on contact. Mother's unwavering
heart. Rickshaw rides to little stores with mother and moon. 2001. Learning

the word insomnia in a Bangla poem. Studying *Pather Panchali* with father. Learning
about a little boy burning his comics and burying his radio before leaving another country.

1969. The little boy, going hungry before exams. The little boy, surrendering his passport.
About being unafraid of darkness because they had to blacken windows to be safe. Aunts,

or their stunted sufferings. The changing length and colour of Anandapuri grass.
Things I can't distil are things that come back in circles. Perhaps I ought

to take a leaf out of my father before he was a father. At fifteen, killing a frog,
then boiling it in a saucepan of calcium hydroxide to extract the skeletal structure

to find out if, after everything had left the frog's body, the bones would stick.

THEY HAVE MORE TO SAY

Mud on their mandibles, the wasps
are carrying around my anger –
expensive black limiting the gold.
I am chewing paper, processing
letters claiming that, put in the wrong
compartment, these part-bee part-ant
creatures of summer can bring down
aeroplanes. The wasps take earth to air
and build their stalactite organ pipe
where they will choose to birth stingers,
daughters over sons, who are expected
to live for a year aculeate in half slumber
and answer to the name *marginata*.

CARRYING AROUND MY ANGER

The heart of linearity was shaken
by waterfalls, but the ants claimed
back the territory. Now, they're bent
on claiming the straightness of my
house. Fortified, formic, they feel
no threat from open taps, bottled
chemicals, plastic slippers, nothing
hurts their egos. Unlike flies, their
eyes don't multiply, but skirt around
every obstacle, seeing none but the ant
in front of them. The ants are taking
quorum, talking loud with catapult
jaws that run in tandem. They have
developed their own code that works
the way molecules bond in hive mind
to turn saccharine. They think they know
what I am thinking. Carrying a planet
each on their shoulders, they're annexing,
building a solar system away from aphids,
my feet and other small disasters. What
does it mean to hit the nail on the head?

OTHER SMALL DISASTERS

The silverfish will drown in water, yet he was not granted wings. He took to reading, first discount coupons and then fiction which was when he started dreaming about a world where the arthropods would wake up to be humans with breasts and fingernails. *How does the eyeless silverfish know when he isn't dreaming?* So, he eats what he reads to make living palpable in starch, relishing on words ending with –ing because then he feels like he is doing something. He wants to cram whole books from cover to end paper, suck marrow from spine, but all he can do in this non-dream insectarium is perforate tributaries that dry up. Inebriated with print, the silverfish sometimes revels in his invertebrate essence and professes lust to the dictionary. But held in a close embrace, he is pressed into becoming a character unfulfilled who can be scraped off the sheet with a flick. He wants to be ink but turns aberrant, wants to be legible, turns into a blot.

SUCK MARROW FROM SPINE

The tautology of termites is affecting
their bodies, turning them invisible,
albino non-nymphs, they show no mercy:
they will digest whole canvases, chairs,
the rosewood chest, gnaw at your heirloom
and still keep mumbling – they have more
to say. They hide inside your bedpost
to eavesdrop pillow talk, but confronted
they escape into nuptial rain, leaving behind
everything but the core: their wings even
the unsaid powdered for you to decipher, but
there is no money in the history of termanium.
It has all been said before: the world is hollowed
out, you did not foresee that they would leave,
wish you had planned a forest in time, wish you
were less porous like heartwood, dead but still solid.

MNEMONIC
on turning twenty-one

It started with matchboxes. On my first collectible, I
Recall a black ship sailing; so on the second, its twin found
En route to school. I traded in duplicates. With time,
Memorabilia changed to notebooks. I collected in between:

Eagle's feathers, silver wrapping paper, phone numbers,
Magnets, and all those letters addressed to you. Rhyming
Billets-doux, confessionals, pieces of my mind and heart
Engraved in red: juvenilia spilling over the borders.

Realizing that age calls for gravity, it was pebbles
That I started collecting, from everywhere I travelled. I
Had this glorious vision of an old woman me,
Insoluble by a grey sea, skipping stones at dawn.

Sacrilegiously I have packed away the thingamajigs. In
Memories I trade, to deserted islands I ship them away.
En fete, I made a bonfire with the fire hoarded inside
Matchboxes and those letters to send smoke signals your way.

Evocative objects these feathers, names of streets have
No real use, they are not magic spells. Penchants
Turn redundant before she who collects souls.
Objects with my fingerprint, address, phone number,

My name: nothing will pin me to this earth. Death catches
Our souls with a butterfly net. The pebbles I gave back to the
River. At its bottom, my collection grows, grows moss.
I collect boulders now, all things that have weight.

IF YOU LOOK LONG ENOUGH

No such event: only a lake approaching us
as we bowed down to its water, undeniably wet,

but not as happy as the dogs who come to lap
the shores every day. The lake does not know us yet.

But it allows the sharp blue dragonfly to make tiny grazes
on its surface. Something moves in the dry mass of bramble

on the other side. An animal perhaps, or just the wind.
We make no guesses; it could be either of the two

and nothing would change. The lake turns dark with knowledge,
this we are sure of, a fact, for one of the dogs starts barking.

Fact upon fact, but what else can nourish us? Even as a swan
cuts through the disc that is the sun, the lake gathers itself

around to heal it whole again. Hidden in lies or glorified in truth,
we have come to the point where we will say nothing new. The animal

or the wind stirs. And there, the lake is acknowledging us. Still, no event.

HOW TO BREED LILACS

First, learn not to stereotype months, then walk
on all fours, sniffing the garden soil, stop at the warmest
patch of earth. Then, dig. Dig deep, delve with love, do not
use a shovel, dig until your ankles are covered, upturn minerals
until the earthworms tickle your toes. Always use your hands,
for everything. Watch out for the microscopic snails who leave
behind trails, softer than your fingers make. If you have powdered
bones, sprinkle them, with ceremony, without hurting others.
Calcium works faster than singing softly to growing plants. Plant
the tiny, the new, the world-condensed-in-a-grain-full-of-potential
seeds. Another piece of advice: do not use adjectives unless you
need them. So, revised: plant those seeds. Use more water for libation,
nothing else purifies, nothing else soaks the soil, mixing memory
and desire. Afterwards, wash your fingernails clean, return
to the kitchen, make yourself a cup of tea. Again, you will find the uses
of water. Cup in hand, sit down by the window, you will see the seeds
bursting out, the roots travelling in tunnels deeper than your reach.
Then, you will see the branches growing: spreading out, those grey
brown birds, reaching towards everywhere, you will see lilacs
clustering, each petal singular, designed with your fingerprints.

YOUR SUCCULENTS NEED A DROUGHT

Once I held a magnifying glass against streaming light and found a single dust particle smiling. Hours spent alone in a house: this is how the world unclothed in front of me. Windows are for winding. Those who accuse me of speaking too little have not met the effusive child of afternoons. Lacks are remedied by invention, so crows and jades and ants invented languages I could understand. In the same way, as if doing them a favour, I grew attached to the desert plants my parents kept bringing home. Saturdays are for pruning. Forgetful gardener, pass on the shears. Yellow our cuticles. A discarded bathtub, full of lotuses, vanished. Or, was carried away by crows from our rooftop. There are some facts you hear for the first time and never forget. Fruit flies share nearly sixty per cent of our DNA. My father told me this when I was fifteen. Giant cycad whorls and whorls and can never be displaced. Here is where I say something about rooting, but there are seasoned gardeners who might be listening. Have you lined the pot bottom with pebbles, have you covered the compost tub? Remember: every drop of water you add to the soil will remain there. Forgetful gardener, is there a hole in your heart? Trees may have a heartbeat that is so slow we never noticed it. In my grandmother's house, the gourd grows and grows, taking over the washing lines. This perhaps will be our lives: to watch plants take over us. The day the doves accepted the nest my mother built for them, someone tried to break into our house. From planting nails to broken pieces of mustard oil bottles, our neighbours kept trying to make their boundary walls impossible to climb over. A crow never forgets the face that has harmed. The gourd peeps ripe through. Shards of glass. On the dining table, next to the place mat, a fishbone turning opaque white. Relentless we want water to pour, but forewarned, and at seasonal intervals. Serrated fruit knife. Forgetful gardener, protect your eyes. My father found a dead civet next to the tub with lotuses. Was it poisoned next door or carried in by kites? For years, one crow would bury bread and bones next to our bonsai peepul. Perhaps this was life: to let birds leave behind their things among our things, so that they keep coming back. The mynahs could not understand the use of the bird feeder, so then the wasps found a way in and are building their nest. When they arrived, the doves had no sense of slope and laid their eggs on plain surfaces. What is the protocol of saving one animal from another's jaws? If there is no eating involved? Forgetful gardener, pebble your heart. Deprived of water for the week that we were away, the jade leaves fattened up for a bleaker future. If ever I go missing, keep looking at rooftops. All night, the helicopter hovered overhead. How many hours of practice before you can fly in the dark? Remind me how moths adapted their bodies to avoid being eaten by bats. So many things fly and fight in the dark while we sleep. This, of course, is all of life: to eat and to avoid being eaten. Forgetful gardener, your neem grows because a mynah ate those neem fruits. Forgetful gardener, you eat like a bird. Do you remember how you once chewed pomegranate seeds and buried them in every flowerpot? To bury is to hide or to forget or to save for the future. To bury is not always nourishment for dear earth. Remember, cold water for blood. Climbing up the stairs, I have forgotten what it was I meant to retrieve. This has happened to me ever since I turned ten. They had to weed out one hundred pomegranate saplings because we are not even home for more than half the year. Miserable, the ulcer dog. Forgetful gardener, the cactus is your heart. And your succulents need a drought. Forgetful gardener, oh what would you grow if you had a square inch of land. There were things I was told to retrieve. Forgetful gardener, the pipes dry up, our soil cracks, what will you love from the desert this time?

DIM LIGHT

Not a degree of brightness but a thing
shaped by soot, glassed by kerosene,
this egg or eggplant-bellied chimney lamp
would be set down by my grandmother
as soon as the lights went out – on table-tops,
bathroom shelves, stairway corners – and being
set down it would conjure fist-finger dogs, doves
in flight without feather, crickets with legs
full of song, against the backdrop of some garrulous
frogs. What is remarkable is not how, if a storm
hits the electric poles, I will automatically recall
the dim light's perfect curvature, but that I cannot
simply remember where it was stored – behind
which cupboard door that dim light stood when
not in use, where it waited wireless for a darkness;
exposed to the sun, alive, fluid with blue, and how
the dim light would just appear out of nowhere
every time I needed it, like a prayer, but mostly
like the hands that carried it towards me.

PICKLING

Even as she pickles mangoes, grandmother
tells me stories. When she was little, she stole
from piles and piles of mangoes that were left
to dry in the courtyard of her village home.
Embalming mangoes in mulled mustard oil, she tells
me the best of the season must live longer. So each April
she carefully preserves: pickles in glass jars churning,
in the pungent sun turning with black cumin and red chilli
slivers to tickle tongues. Grandfather walks in, always a step
behind his cane, declares the best mangoes grew in our garden,
there, back then. I listen to these stories dipping my finger in
spiced oil: everything on the tip of my tongue. In another city,
eating out of a can I realise that I have not learnt the exact art
of pickling mangoes. I can pickle words, use ink in place of oil.

PORAGHATI

More often than not, love takes the shape of a discoloured harmonium reed
pressed to song for decades, and sometimes love is the memory of a goat,
black with yellow eyes, named Motor, nodding his head to a young girl singing
in Poraghati. Sometimes love is hilarious, though some other times it takes
the shape of places I can never be: the morning my grandmother, the young girl,
hurt herself threshing grains on a dheki, later in bed comforted by the whitest cat
Poteshwari and Colgate her son (named so because, well, his stomach acted like a tube
of toothpaste). Some others: day the mathematics teacher from across the border,
got news of his favourite student, eligible (but we didn't know him then), so just a boy
who would become a physics and maths teacher himself, walking to school
with a magnifying glass, unwittingly burning his big toe. One way to get curious
about the multiplication of light, I suppose. Some things add up, more things don't.
Growing up, because of borders, border towns and not understanding train timetables,
I have lost track of a larger family: where they came from, what districts, how they spent
their evenings. It muddles up, except for the centre: my grandmother and her animals,
who seem to return in silent feet or loud wings outside my door and I let them all in –

★

But not all doors are for opening. When she was hardly ten, for example, near midnight
the dacoits came in armed with sticks, flame torches, their bodies oiled so they could flee,
scattering utensils behind them until they reached the sinduk – there was blood, blows
on the head and the children climbed down a thin drumstick tree to the neighbour's house
but because the branches broke when it came to my great-grandmother, she just flung
herself onto the remaining arms of the tree. This in the darkness of Poraghati, a village
with no electricity, where a few years ago, the young girl's aunt could not complete her sentences
one night, come face to face with a tiger. How many near misses add up to a family? But that's
not all, my grandmother tells me now, we got a donala-gun, my uncle taught all of us how to shoot.
And I have to ask, you too? Of course, she says, it was my duty to clean and stock the shotgun
with two bullets, every night. And when her uncle fell ill, the loaded gun rested above her head.
Another detail: the young girl hid her gold chain under her bed amidst a store of muddied
potatoes. Potatoes! A roar caught in the throat, sometimes love is in the hiding or in the mud.

★

Poraghati: the etymology still in debate, if it was a 'full' or a 'burning' set of stairs leading
to water. Depends on how you open your mouth. There are more details, of course, more
doors, trees, but if you open the panel of the harmonium or feel the air escaping out of its
bellows, you'll find spaces meant not to be filled because how else will there be music?
And now, as soon as my grandmother recalls the details, says must have been borshakal,
there was drizzle that night, and lightning – it starts raining (on a hot April evening) in my
part of the country. Strange and stranger still are the coincidences of love. This I know,
since the time my grandmother encouraged me to write with chalk on red oxide floors –
in the stories I tell, the protagonist is always a girl, friend to all animals,
learning to do everything, ready to fight even on the darkest of all nights.

I LOST TIME SITTING OPPOSITE YOU IN THE LIBRARY

When the book was shut, the pages kissed
a pressed flower. Preserved between print,
the impression of it still —
on page one hundred and six. A stain
saying forget-me-not-lover, on the words:
She is tumbling all treasures of the earth at her feet
 — that is the persona of Proust speaking,
by the (Swann's) way, where the petals were found,
veins spilling organic sepia on a yellowing
library book, overdue, for the ninth of December 2011 was yesterday.
Today is the tenth. I turn to find that it was due several decades
ago, on the thirtieth of October 1979, and then, again, and again,
in winter months, twenty-two out of twenty-nine
borrowed times. Winter, I decide, is the season of
remembrance. Remembrance. It is a word like the word
fragrance. You want to close eyes, and search for shapes
that you saw as a child before you went to bed.

WHY DID YOU STOP WRITING?

Chaff needs from wants. When my father gives me his old notebook, that earliest lesson he taught comes back. Imagine my shock. At twenty-one, he was writing poetry. I'm trying to translate them, at twenty-five, or more accurately: I'm trying to talk to this young person, my father before he was a father. Between poems titled 'ইউক্যালিপটস, তুমি' and 'পোস্টার', lies a slip. His hostel-room fee. Rupees twenty-five and twenty-three paisa. I imagine him walking the city he's moved to, lingering in corridors, at the TT table, the alley of books, which he would later describe to us as his haunts. He once pointed out his hostel-room window. So, now, when I read the poem he had written about staring out of that gap, from the inside, something happens to the words: কবি হে, বড়ই মুশকিল! What made him write many versions of the same words: নেই রাজ্যের রাজা আমি, বুকের বাঁ দিকে সেলাই করা এক তিনশো চল্লিশ গ্রামের হৃদপিণ্ড? Then, three years ago, he suddenly recited his poem about the Farraka Barrage being built and the slow fade of load-shedding. Across the dark walls, its long title fleeted like a train: 'দ্বাদশীর রাতের চিন্তাগুলি চাঁদ দেখতে দেখতে'... Alongside poems, on the last page of the notebook – some caricatures, and a list: money he owes to friends, largest set aside for *Grey's Anatomy*. A stanza begins in Bangla, but then is taken over by notes on the cortisol, in English. Each poem is dated, phrases scratched out, there are names I don't recognize who sit snug on lines about dreams, pain, hopes and fear. Dressing gowns, pale faces, the smell of blood: his days recur in the poems, and that young poet, at nineteen, asks a lot of questions: কি করে আমরা পরস্পরের ঘ্রাণ নেবো ? কবি হে,

কে বলে বেঁচে থাকার কোনো মানে হয় না? At twenty-one, he could not have known what was to come ten years later, if his poems would survive. Did he care? *Chaff needs from wants*. I look at the endlessness I have been given, can't help but wonder if blindfolded I'd be able to pick stone from rice.

FUTURE LIBRARY: SOME ANXIETIES

stories will be buried like children found dead face down on a beach, words printed today will be read a hundred years from now, but who will have access? lines written

now will take refuge under soil and over them, a forest will keep growing, but in between what if our language capsizes, syllables wobble out of a too-full boat? a hundred years

from now, everything will be different, but tonight stories will be taken to undisclosed locations, stories will be rendered speechless, or declared a threat to internal security,

stories will be coerced, stopped at the border, or be photoshopped to look like someone else, stories will be in possession of firearms, stories will be blinded by pellets, stories will

overhear a hypodermic's confession to needles, stories will forget their beginnings, and in forgetting, will eat other stories, but then a hundred years from now things may be different.

while a thousand trees are growing, they said: we are not interested in your information, we are not interested in your gene pools, in your lives lived without passwords, without a common

currency of manufactured teeth marks. stories will be told to put the arctic to bed and tuck in polar bears under a warm blanket, stories will wonder what other forests can home them. stories

will google: dandakaranya. białowieża. juruá-purus. stories will look for patterns in stories about forests which are often stories of exile and often end in fire. stories will stop believing

that stories are endangered when they go to the mall and see a polar bear lift his head to the camera, stories will say extra cheese on pizza but say, a hundred years from now, will our

children still be reading? will knowledge still be bitten in fruits or like vitamins, sealed in pills? stories will google: earth, google translate: earth. stories, say: foliage, say: moon, scribble love

on palms or sit by our caves but stories will refuse, for tonight stories will go to war, stories will take the storyteller hostage a hundred years from now, how lovely that then we will all be gone

SALT

We sit at the table passing around the blame.
No one takes a slice. An animal tries to warn
us, but we have her for dinner. We were hungry.
Tomorrow we will warm up the leftovers.
We wait for water. A few hours without it
is terrible but we have been told that the body
will adjust. For now, a sandstorm in the throat
but later certain, like bark. One of us is convinced
that she is no longer an animal. More veins, less
blood. We avoid looking at the tall glass with stems
of cut flowers. Unseasonal heat. Our impatient children
stick their fingers into the peach to prize out a stone.
A centre so hard you'd feel lucky to find rings instead
of ribs and where her toes were before, a complication
of roots. Shoot nothing from your mouth but a calm
that confirms not all rainfall is benediction. Imagine
this: a sanitary kitchen, windows, tiles, spoons made
of wood and a row of potted plants, stomata sparkling
like salt. That dawn was chlorophyll stained. Her wants
become simpler: air, liquid, light. No, don't imagine this;
become a paradox so clean it cannot be touched. Let us
compare the sharpness of wives. We have not come far,
it is the forest that recedes farther away from our reach.
Another animal tries to warn us, we can feel our teeth
growing warm. Our reluctance goes cold. Afterwards,
we will paint our grief.

LIKENESS
OR
AM I ALWAYS SAYING TOO MUCH

Months like March, I can't bring myself
to take photographs. Instead of frozen frames of you
lying next to your dog, treading waves, admiring melons,
I give you, to press between palms or poems, some names
of plants in your father's garden in my mother tongue:
lobongolotika, noyontara, kathtagore, madhabilata, kanchan

★

You halve a *bimbli* into a simmering pot. Analyzing the fruit the way
my mind always tries to fish for a science lesson, a simile, a pattern
to dilute the shock of encountering something startlingly new this late
in life, I spout: *bimbli* is an elongated *amla*. You sprinkle salt and say
it's not as caustic and I have to utter the word *kosh* which in Bangla means
almost the same thing, then go on cleaning the back of my teeth with *saban*,
so close to *savon* little delights lather up and yet, nothing surprised me more
than the sudden appearance of mangroves when we were driving on a pitch
road between clumps and clumps of breathing roots over cool clearwater

★

Your books, your candles, your silver fish in perfect order
I have always watched you with a wild wonder and now you say
here is where I feel most alive barefoot roaming the grounds at dawn.
I wonder if I have finally come to Socorro to write that one poem
that must be written for you because how else can I say it, wild:
seven years ago, when you threw the universe out of a window,
some of it fell into my hands. Is there only one month *like* March?

★

Are the names of flowers more beautiful than the flowers?
More permanent? The whirl of the ceiling fan and I can spend hours
at your bay window where a sunbird tries to break into light – it's not
like the sunbird wants to be solar, but our language desires an opulence
or a translucency which I project onto my love for our ecosystem, or
my fears

★

Here there are marigold garlands around crosses. I readjust
my sight to the many construction work notices on tin. High
noon. We're soaking in old neighbourhoods, the symmetry
of traditional Portuguese tiles. I recite what little I have come
to know about them arriving here in 1501 from a book I have
been editing: historical fiction in translation, compressed for our
English-language readers, so it's hard to count the number of
times I feel removed from it all and it hits me: the word violence
is dangerously close to the word opulence & Here is a language
I don't remember hearing before, and because I have heard
so little of it I will not be able to recognize it when I hear it
again & Here are the permanent gaps between us all & Here
is a bulldozer hacking away at the red earth of your hometown,
revealing roots, nothing but roots & Here

★

are a few other freeze frames, if you move through them quickly enough they acquire motion:
you storming into the rooms drawing curtains chanting *too bright too bright*. From the middle
of March starts the last month of the Bangla calendar, did you know? *Choitro*

almost like *chitro* meaning image, a likeness, like *cholochitro* meaning moving pictures

★

My displaced memory of a steel wind turbine near a cliff with white statues
versus you and your friends refuting its existence: almost the same thing.
You scowl at a photograph and say *I have never liked this taint of summer*
and when I ask you if you meant tint, you fluff a pillow and say *English
is a language just waiting to be distorted*. Soon after – I trip over kaju nuts, grass
shoots up from our hips, thoughts braid, bread rises to become *pui,* there are
lattices, no, there is laterite, or hollows visible on earth where the creek meets
the sea, molluscs, *mohona*, pineapple, giant red moon, palm fronds fall, the universe
clings to panes, blades slice the air, isn't forgetting almost the same thing as us all
flowing through some sluice which is really pipes or wires or nerves carrying water,
agua, agun, again, sprinklers, *kalboishakhi*, scraping leftovers, perhaps the garden knows

HAZARDOUS

is walking the streets
without glasses
thinking
the world is/the world is looking

        so out of focus pretty as in those *[insert name of city]*
        I Love You movies festooned with lens flares that are
        speeding headlight asterisks growing bigger or smaller
        falling leaves or number plates turning into hats/heads
        of pedestrians/limbs superimposed the camera follows
        the protagonist's eyes looking out for blackbirds/a sign

is fidgeting with the frame
or trying to fluff up the thinness
of these days by saving every bus ticket

        only to crumple them into flowers crushed handmade
        for that everbasket in the corner already overflowing
        with last month's list of groceries/library due dates/
        amassing clues to remember in case all is lost in trans-
        actions or in case the next thermal paper questionnaire
        asks *who would you like to have as your dinner guest?*

DREAM ARGUMENT

chipmunk chatter is to birdsong, so we take
long walks when it thunders
                 and I'm still cocooned, too thin,
and yes, nothing is random, everything is history,
the future is or will be – bottom's up – a peacock
        emerging in shorts from your balcony
sometimes I feel nilgai and of course, this poem
                 has no use nor is
                 important
but I'd like it to become a sincere shade of blue –
yes, change will come, yes, we too will
                                         change
and of course, the world is bigger and stranger than us all
and of course, to pay attention is not necessarily to be kind
and of course, I'm full of pretences and you're sceptical
                 but mostly you're patient
even with the trivial (because maybe the trivial will save us)
        like my reluctance to chew fish-heads
        a moment scrawled on a paper napkin
        between silly solipsism and the science
        of soot sprites
let us balance kittens – no, kettles – on our heads,
keep flinging questions until the great hive breaks,
perhaps this poem could be your dream
                        of my being a moth
in the corner of the ceiling –
for what are we when we're not, or where

NORTH DELHI, WINTER

The walls are thick with whitewash here
but when the smog climbs in, it is difficult
to tell which layer you can pass through.

That overhead bulb is switched on all the time,
even at night, one must convince oneself: light
is warmth, warmth is light,

but before sleep is heavy, shut the window tight
lest you wake up while it's still dark and mistake
it for the door you always wanted to travel through.

In two months, deprived of water, the bougainvillea will
take over, so for now, let us hoard all the pinecones we can.

They are burning leaves in the afternoon to smoke up
the space between us, you are leaving, saying

this smog never promised to cushion your fall.

SETTING
for children's books illustrators

These are those landscapes of books read during summer holidays these are those landscapes in stories about other summer holidays but here are the landscapes within my reach I am walking through but I cannot name every tree but sometimes one slips out of my mouth a flash in brown and blue like the jay who visits my window every afternoon who will perch on the same branch birch sycamore oak dogwood suspecting acorns or a fox among berries who turns out to be a roe deer too close to the highway and so they are all here now but long ago I would spend afternoons wondering how soft foxgloves would be to touch in the sharp of a certain wind for the pages of the borrowed school library books were more or less the same degree of papery although during the first months this nearness filmed over as an elsewhere and what I saw of England I saw in ink sketches in pencil lined pages on the opposite sides of stories.

TRAINING MY EAR: A JOURNAL

New Delhi, Week 1, 2010

Two phones. Two voices.
One conversation that I'm not part of.
Malayalam sounds like
Japanese. On days I'm full watching anime.
Kimi ni todoke. Though sometimes like
French. On days that smell concrete of poetry.
Si Tu Savais. My roommate is on the phone again.
She cracks a joke. I can hear his laugh.
He teases. She blushes. On this side of the line.
They talk for hours. *Sorry* in English is
the only word I can make out.
Sorry, I shouldn't be listening.

Coventry, Week 2, 2013

Again I have taken to listening to conversations
I don't understand, languages I will never learn;
I tell myself that this eavesdropping
is for research only, perhaps it will
generate some poetry, language begets
language and – immediately the world
swells up, and I begin to see how syllables
can bounce out of toasters, or are dropped delicately
to dissolve in tea cups, how vowels fall through
the fine holes of a colander, phrases you want
to swallow whole made of sounds that shine,
a globule of light at the end of spoons, those
bits of table talk I try very hard to catch between
my fingers or chopsticks, delicious amateur nothings

PAPER SONG

It took me nine hours of crammed knees to reach here, nine hours
of watching countries become gridlines on a screen to reach eight

hundred miles away from Barrackpore, but finally, I can pin down
why I feel at home in a stranger's room in Nuneaton: a child's drawing

of a baul in a patchwork overall; behind him, coconut trees sway their pastel
leaves to the crayon ektara that makes music in the form of trembling lines

radiating like the rays of the corner sun that looks more like an orange; a lone
lotus floats on the edge of the paper pond, and the road on which this minstrel

walks, eyes closed forever, is wide and red and brown and –
starts from the horizon in fat finger strokes, does not end even when the paper ends

BY A DIFFERENT LINE

Incomprehensible this May morning you wake up
from one dream   *blood in your mouth*   to walk into
another. Sometimes the absence of a verandah the slope
of all rooftops gets too much, you wonder how even
after the sun has   long hit   the undersides of leaves
the daisies still curl their tiny white tongues at your feet
dandelion clocks are frosted over and refuse to disperse
on the highway you stop reading the signs and fix your
energies on overhead   vapour trails   *this could be anywhere*
(*why, Coventry?*) but the tropical is trapped inside a glasshouse
looking exotic even to you where is the corridor that ends
in wilderness, but everywhere is *nowhere lit up* so you walk
to the bus stop past all the stores   turning coins   in your
pocket for luck   no one   in sight perhaps *it's just you* who
is stationary this May morning you want to lock yourself
in your room and try waking up again to something more
comprehensible or do you mean *more compassionate*   had it not
been for the timely intervention that inevitability of *birdsong*

HARE'S BREATH

I am still getting used to this new neighbourhood.
There are birds, the heat does not leave the stones.

No, this will not do. To speak to you I need
new words for: dreams, language, kaleidoscope,
but the irony sits in the middle. On the final day,
your key was in my pocket. A fact so simple
I could cry. I want to write to you, but I am trying
to understand why I worry more than I love. We
could be somewhere else, but look at me, I am still
here thinking up animals, their faces so close you
could touch their voice. Perhaps you can see them.

Does all waiting end in an appearance? Surely not.

You told me that I will never know what happened
in the last ten years, to you that is, it made me sad,
we watched
a film without subtitles.

My made-up animal has met you in a parallel world,
in a country obscure to us, where the importance
is in not knowing. The trouble is with time, yes, but let
us not belittle our own inadequacies either.

I want to write to you: *the architecture of my reality*
is failing. But it is too hot here. The stones refuse
to leave the birds. The neighbourhood greys.

I still want to write to you, but we are doing other things.
Something else will happen, we have seen the key turn,
the shapes change.

FUTURE LIBRARY: A FOOTNOTE

no children for me – when I said *our* – I really meant the collective world's; no children for me because I am not the fittest and I dislike Sundays for the same reasons I decline syrup or because flowers like hydrangea, daliah, marigold make me uneasy.

        Mummy, have we ever thought as a species?

xerox, xylem, xylophone, phonetic, phony – it's an alphabet of losing sensation: first earlobe, then shin. I hide behind the cryptic but tell me, is fitness mathematical? meanwhile, superbugs, meanwhile, planets with atmospheres, meanwhile, dinosaur eggs, meanwhile, bodies burnt, culpability framed, meanwhile, a new mall, meanwhile, the sneer slant of spring saying hello, meanwhile more pills, or we measure our lives with expiry dates, meanwhile, the slow cancellation of our futures, meanwhile, nerve gas, meanwhile on the phone, in the next cubicle: are you sure it will translate to sales?

I don't mean a thing in matter – pleasure texture textual pressure – but let's cultivate nurturing in a petri dish. lover beloved = mother child? hexagonal rooms, protein sequence browser history: foetus attempts to manipulate maternal physiology and metabolism for foetal benefits. mummy, was I as selfish? let omissions be only accidents, coded information convincing us that a nest is an extended phenotype, that a healthy body is whole. the probability of being replicated with errors is at times attractive but I am predictable.

        Mummy, what is the evolutionary incentive for lying?

a hundred years from now maybe we'll no longer need to dream a dream of the nuchal cord or maybe our self-pollinating heads will solve these problems – what's more optimal? I only believe in the body which feels pain. say, a hundred years from now, under those trees in the forest we are growing, will there still be children *reading*?

                                          Text me when you reach home.

IS IT COLD OR AM I TIRED OF THE DUST?

A bleak afternoon drags out the worst
in me. Thoughts of leaving appear
as easily as sleep, and refuse to be rubbed
off. The eyes travel lazily: trampled on
for a week, the onion skin has turned
mosaic, indistinguishable from the floor.

He says I could do much more than describe
events that happen to no one else, or where
nothing happens, yet I keep repeating; I want
to ask him why we don't witness our daily
decay more closely, but a different question
takes over – am I selfish for spending
an entire day cleaning a room where I live alone?

Who can I speak for with conviction? To save
a little potted plant, I severed its head, buried
the dead leaves in its soil. I won't see it happen,
but soon it will all become spectacular, green.

POSSIBLY OCTAGONAL

Three Sundays later, four
eyes are confronting eight
boxes, seven lids, or one
mynah is startled by glass.

Yesterday was moving
five years from floor
one to floor three.
A useful exercise.

And today, the morning
is nothing but leaves guessing
the shape of light.

How many corners?
A question followed
by another white night.

Then, simply looking,
or looking away.
No numbers, no pain.

IT IS COLD, AND I AM TIRED OF THE DUST

There is no epiphany at the end of this poem. This is not
a confession either, or an experiment to find out if words can
pin the ephemeral. To watch a male seahorse change colour
and give birth is a way to pass time or a way to realise I don't want
to be the person who says I've been watching the animals, but they
are not doing anything. For years, I've been watching my own legs
freeze inside natural history museums every time it's just me and them.
Each of us gazing. Out of glass, out of glass eyes. I've been watching
time lapse videos of coral reefs. We were there once, spitting on goggles,
unable to fathom the purple from the future grey. Is this why we can't be
both dew and gravel? There is no sharp turn in the middle of this poem.
Only a desire to open the windows, only to realise how I write of trees,
but have not yet stepped out, out of the garden yet. To witness is not enough,
what do I know of the fire in bellies, or, of the cold outdoors? The hills are
frowning and all this happens in languages we cannot read, nor write. Unable
to fathom if, by we, I mean this-is-an-attempt-to-fortify-the-lonely-future-I.
Closing anthers, shifting pines. Speak then in river vanishing, or speak with
gaping beak, because to sing or to sigh is not enough either, and to heal – well,
I strayed that path long ago, so, like other beloved truths, this too is hard to admit,
but like truths that are difficult to own and dear to keep, I know this as I take
one last look at your hawk-swell eyes, your cradle-wood arms, I know this as
you move out of sight: I will never be able to love this earth as much as you do.

AT 2 A.M., I CONFLATED EVERYONE AND EVERYTHING

Our greed is bulbous.
A house inside a house inside a house. Switchboards collapsing.
Fingers frantic for the matchbox as soon as the wires snap.

The weight of one body cancels out the missing weight of another.
Almost. One of us observes this from the outside.
One of us, yearning for a ghost.

A black jaguar and a black wolf walked beside you while I slept.
The morning was swallowed whole until my teeth felt my other teeth.
The future floated out from the past.

Lunch?
Yes.
This is the loneliest exchange I've had with my most beloved.

We managed our sadness well. Painted vegetables made of earth.
A diary of accounts. A dead butterfly mounted at least thirty years ago.
Unflapping blue wings. Deep or dark, the web.

Incurable: the way my body will match the breathing of the body next to me.
Somewhere, two mirrors fog in sync to suggest we are alive.
During sun shower, foxes everywhere are falling in love.

Out of fallacies and ambiguities, another day, another child will be born.
We will continue to misunderstand each other.
At 2 a.m., confused, a crow will laugh.

And then, just like that, you start telling me a story.
And then, just like that, I begin to see some specifics more than some others:
blue around the eyes, a damp mouth, damp hair, a keen neck.

We are alive. Typed out: *Yes*. Haunting, this simple affirmation.
In a language we never speak, but did that day, out of a different kind of loneliness.
It's summer again. We know how it will end.

For now, I can say this, so let me: you make it so easy,
to grow into your measured and unhurried tenderness, so easy
and so difficult to wake up and leave behind dreams, their endless charity.

FUTURE LIBRARY: ALTERNATIVE ENDING

the opposite of dystopia
        is ~~not utopia~~,
    ~~possible, compassion,~~ unprejudiced
          participation

     stories will be passed on
         despite nations conspiring to be selectively inherited,

stories will remember every other story,
stories will be scavenged from threadbare dialects,
stories will be translated, stories will
        rise up from mass unmarked graves to confront
          the hypocrisy
            of storytellers,

stories that breathe underwater will gather on top of each other like spider crabs
    to discard their old shells and grow softly
    into themselves, into themselves bigger,
breathing through masks and armed with watering cans, stories in your neighbourhood
    will make a comeback
      like the saiga antelope,
      fill the sky
      with screeches like an echo parakeet,
          stories will stop sitting on fences, stories will ferry
cures, after counting 915 coins from the stomach of a turtle,
        stories will give up on miracles
          and take matters into their own hands,

stories will
    disown gods,
      escape frameworks, mouths, the market,
        stories will never figure out how they end,
          how lovely then that we'll be able to say we had a hand in this.

15 AUGUST 2017

I will tell you what was blaring from the microphones
that day my brother and I, on a rickshaw, trying to reach –
we shall overcome – past old neighbourhoods when I made note
of the old coconut tree still shooting through red rooftop tiles
of the bicycle shed, and then I will tell you that we were –
trying, but we did not reach – some six or seven minutes late.

I will tell you which flowers were on his bedsheet and which of his
students came as soon as they heard and what stories they remembered.
I will tell you how the neighbours marvelled when they heard how he
had not said a final word, nor shown any signs that morning, only
asked that *rabindrasangeet* played on; they said that was because he had led
a good, honest life, that was the proof from this uncomplicated death –

If you ask me how the night passed in that house, I will tell you to go ask
my brother, my mother, my aunt and my grandmother, who were there with him;
when I went again the next morning, the two white cats came for breakfast
as if nothing had changed. So did the buses, trains, airplanes and taxis, they all arrived,
mostly on time and then everyone he had long wanted to see together was suddenly
in the same room, facing the small difference of an empty chair and she said how happy
he would have been at this miraculous gathering. Because you did not ask, I will tell you all

this while, from then to now, has been a slow caving in. Between phone calls and this evening
on the rooftop, good old disbelief. And some moths. In Barrackpore, can you imagine that
gulmohar grandfather planted still in bloom, and the stubborn coconut tree swaying in
a triumph beyond our reach. I will tell you everything I can remember just so you can tell me
what to do with all these words, these hours or years folded into sentences that grow longer
and yet, in these twenty-six breeze years, never being able to console another. Only marvelling
at the fine-tuning of crepuscular grief, then luring towards me this soft child of air and abyss

DINOSAUR ON WHEELS

BONSAI to begin with we kill too much or grow too little, that which is alive without asking for much should always be kept alive, if we can figure out how time fills in trees perhaps we will be able to build our time machine

STETHOSCOPE a most intimate knowledge is the only world we were raised to believe in, everything else plain brass painted with hands, hot when heated otherwise cold, a magnification of cause event and exception, the smell of comfort is a lab coat hanging among saris, an explanation of the heart as a congregation of fears in the artery

VELVET LINING inside an unused jewellery box where we collected dead mosquito bodies for a few weeks, questions and laughter now piling up into a tiny country of the forgotten with maybe a coastline that glistens every time a dormant memory washes ashore

EXHAUST FAN the second in the bathroom to quicken bodies and to disperse traces of Sunday soap and cigarettes while the first in the nude light of a soft sieved kitchen whirls to announce our morning tea

CLOTHESLINE a limitation, liberated from which the towels now dry could have aimed for the stars this moment in May nothing more exquisite than the rain, indoors we play name place animal thing and bet on the shrinking of constellations as soon as they are named

UNDER THE BED paper or a stain that multiplied and introduced herself as Stein, I am your temporary object of devotion, conversation about someone else could put an end to this futile reconstruction, but not everyone wants to talk in language a fluctuating necessity like a mosquito net, sometimes let's take it slow and remember our power cut terrace summoning fireflies

AQUARIUM gathers dust then is a support for a bird cage, but the civet sneaks in through the pipe and there are feathers floating; a study in plastic is an underwater cherub pissing to entertain fishes, later used to showcase dolls neglected but tall to the knees, rectangular breathing that might as well predict a restricted range of affect or what was soon spelt out to be tachycardia

ATTIC cannot be reduced to a poem because a tiger dwells there or so everyone made the children believe and the children believed because the place seemed to be big enough for the tiger and yes sometimes its darkness moved making the time machine sing

MIRROR opposite which stands another mirror this is as loud as the wish for infinity can get, call it lateral envy and stay still then lean sideways out of the frame to see hands after hands after hands waving smooth takeovers the thing moving in thermometers a night of high fever that was when kitten died many kittens died many kittens turned into cats only to die something about love beyond death and a lapse into cliché a nausea for nostalgia but no a cloying clock never works endless images so detailed I think they are last night's dream THERE ARE FACES I WANT TO REMEMBER but my elsewhere syndrome won't let the world's present be pinned on to my present which is really a myth

TV TABLE which is the preserved root of a tree painted as black as the bordering floor some imitation flowers now discarded instead fresh limes from the tree are kept there to go with the nine o'clock news

SHOECASE a constant fear of forgetting one evening she slipped on her feet my tiny white sandals and tried to run away that's what they said but maybe she only wanted to take a walk impossible to explain why next year I placed my leg over the balcony railing though this is what I had said then: because the metal was so cool and I wanted to feel the coolness against the skin at the back of my knee, such accuracy of desire has evaded me since, every time we went on a vacation, I became a different person leaving a ghost of a girl in tourist towns still dizzy with the world enlarging; it might have been a crisp evening who was to know

MEZZANINE difficult to spell and terrible to count, she feels smothered on birthdays and pushes away their recurrence; whoever can recall what the other cannot has stakes: siblings with memory as sharp as elephants, memory in the singular, still sliding down a banister in a house we cannot go back to where I would not think before feeling

SPIT BALLS or the art of aiming chewed newsprint to the ceiling or the philosophy of keeping details of bad news out of reach or the science behind our imprinting forever things that happen only once like buying two ten-rupee tickets to see strange wonders suspended in formaldehyde and the calf with two heads gently nibbling hay inside the last tent at the February fairground

GIGANTIC GLASS JAR of puffed rice stored for shitstorm evenings chai chai chai the want of every hand kept fresh with a red screwcap, always there behind the sliding cupboard door until it broke of course but by then it was clear that no one has ever solved the mathematics of smaller tragedies and listing the dead obliquely won't bring them back either; if only places were easy to forget if only people did not make those places so easy to remember

REFRIGERATOR DOOR magnets holding crayon rockets and stegosaurus a preoccupation with creatures unable to walk this earth any more like our cat singing to coriander what is a relief is that this world enlarges for someone else now, even now, even as you see it shrinking, there is a dinosaur on wheels riding the streets of your arms, encountering scabs and bumps and bones anew

BOX OF BUTTONS and several other emergencies have crossed over to the realm of the surreal numbered as the nineties: smoking a snake out at night was not unusual nor crying eyeballs out over a hand-stitched rabbit; books the only enduring totems but then everything and everyone who let light shine through them turned wondrous because we had not come to the realization that would eventually kill PEOPLE NEVER MEAN WHAT THEY SAY decades later trying to decipher a shape in a January jacket that seems to have emerged from gaps between my obsession with childhood landscapes, an antidote to the clawing of clocks decades later a chronic who are you *But many facts about a life should be left out, they are easily replaced* – with what with what with what

CORRESPONDENCE
for my friends, for writing back

This February light lilts a kite's screech – the sound of abandonment *No ink in the world* you wrote last November *bleeds through this paper* and now I don't even know what to say How could all that snow take over all those trees in Rostanga But really, how warm are your feet tonight How far are you year after year away from your home your family How tired I tried but there was – *I hope this reaches you before you leave* I tried but things fell through mud baths, naphthalene balls, winter drawer of knives, three foxes in the sun I did not mean to say so many things out of the blue that mean so much else As soon as I write it all down for you I'm preparing to forget Do you ever feel that way *Let's keep going We'll get somewhere The only things you can say* Your tongue trying to roll out Swahili, on a day it rains here, no, pours, and on a street corner someone shivers: I know it's not you Because the last time I saw you when geography was kind and we had somehow appeased time We were running on the streets, after a bus We were trying to climb down a rooftop Constructing an unbearable future tense We were stuck We were sitting on a mound and those black balloons like grapes appeared and disappeared overhead We were absurd Passing on reading lamps and chilli plants We picked up a map Were we watching seals Café No 33 There was a body of water You were singing outside my door In V's room wasn't the chandelier swaying Therefore *this can't be good but it is it is* the kite's screech is not the sound of abandonment A convincing mix of choice and coincidence where can I get *I walk a lot these days* I am trying to understand Subject: the moon is a scythe tonight and the sky is bruised blue Subject: why are a male sparrow's eyes stamped with grief Subject: how do we counter misplaced mass hate Subject: it's been a long time Subject: am I a fool to dwell on the recurrences of ruins, hotels, tigers in my dreams Subject: is it impossible to rebel in quietude *Where are we now? I hardly know! In Kerry, of course In Delhi* Haunted afternoons, who was that talking her heart out to a sparrow: saying I want to be littler, unnoticeable, flit in and out of rooms *Things said in abundance can become meaningless* December ending, something about humility, or the soil under your shoes Old questions *should we have –* Or eating lunch at my desk, someone hands me an envelope and it's you from across the sea declaring you are in love, in love *it's always five o'clock here* Disguised as the weather, a fact about bee-eaters Marginal bloom May not reach *I'm looking forward to the future, are you?* Your skyline handwriting Don't worry Years ago *tomar postcard peye ami bhoyanok khushi* I know it's not enough and I don't know what else is but I think about you every day Then there's the barbet, somewhere very close, oh, oh, oh, the barbet drilling my head And, then, there's you, with the endless questions and the kind eyes, you, here, impossibly close: you, how are you?

ERRATA

In this collection, the most frequent noun is the word bird
occurring sixty-six times, followed by story
at forty-five and time *at twenty-eight*

The intention was not to make readers queasy
The intention was to get away and grow up
The intention was to keep moving
The intention was not to lie or to lie beautifully
The intention was to be more worthy and less cardboard
The intention was to never let you say things that you did not mean
The intention was to warn you about earthquakes and thank yous
The intention was not to take your kindness for granted
The intention was to chain stitch questions
The intention was a stranger
The intention had a cervical rib
The intention will never return in delusions or lists
The intention was to fit in your hands
The intention was to let go of a child
The intention was to soap the mouth that said forever
The intention was not to speak indirectly to you all the time
The intention was not to write more than two poems about writing poetry
The intention was to remember everything because everything happened
The intention was to remain invisible unless required otherwise
The intention was to pronounce the word pastiche with flair
The intention was not to take up more space than necessary
The intention was to become somewhat necessary
The intention was and was not flowers
The intention was not to apologise

AND OTHER STORIES

when a bird   ing not to be
when a bird   selfish when
enters a room   a room opens
the window   opens up to
bbbdiesbbb   rrrrbirdsrrrr
a glassy death   says death is

when a glass   a bird trying
when a glass   not to be sel-
enters a bird   fish or trying
the window   not to be glass
iiiisaysiiiii   dddwhenddd
was only try-   a bird enters

BABUI

the weaverbird only confides in your great-grandmother
whose name is another word for the river who wrings
her sari each afternoon and stretches it straight on the line

something so white laid out to dry the weaverbird is prone
to mistaking it for that one story everyone wants to hear
in which the bird saves the farmer boy the old witty way

some say that the weaverbird carries a bit of cow dung
and a few glow worms to make his home visible from
the inside | some say the weaverbird started this rumour |

you want to ask the weaverbird how he keeps the glow
worms alive between the beak but the weaverbird will
not teach you his soft-mouthed craft the weaverbird will

fabricate lies nine yards long and supple enough to pass
through a ring | the weaverbird knows that your family
is waiting for the lift before the glide the call of the sky

so that when they all leave their hollowed out art hanging
from a branch within your reach you will add one more
nest to your collection | find one more room for keeps

TUNTUNI

but it was the tailorbird who taught me to sing
with my mouth closed | to measure each wager
and never to underestimate a person who could
stitch | hiding is difficult if the passion is to sing
the tailorbird said trying out each thread | bombax
windfall to spider's lot settling for a nest of fragrance
amongst nylon vines | the night-blooming jasmine
has sweeter names but summer is dry is a dusk
is a stalk of simpler jasmines on a gunmetal plate
floating on a film of water or dying a slow death
the tailorbird fears the plaintive cuckoo who will
slip in the wrong subplot at a cue meant for someone
else | whatever happens must appear as prevention
or permission | the tailorbird has stationed me where
the roots end and the jasmine tree begins in an undoable
gnarl the eye can't splice where each morning my mother
or my father will add tealeaf mounds that look like upturned
hives to nourish the soil which at night turns into a stage
where everyone must exhibit a song or a skill | so elaborate
a stage the tailorbird left before teaching me the refrain
and a passer-by who I thought was there to listen decides
to speak instead and says – let's face it now this story
will proceed at the will of the one who holds that thread

CHORUI

something about chillies drying in the heat | the crow said yes to the sparrow who challenged that she could digest more grains of wheat than he could chillies what is the prize the crow said and the sparrow said whoever wins will feast on the other bird's heart | the crow asked liver included and the sparrow said fine | the probable tenderness of sparrow liver was better than any carrot and the chillies were gone in no time | the sparrow sighed and said okay but just this is my last wish could you please wash your beak before you touch me no one trusts what you eat and the last thing I want is to be alive yet unclean | so the crow goes to the river but the river says the same thing | the crow thinks all food turns into drops *then our crow goes to the*

potter	jug | scoop water	no clay
bull	horn | dig earth	a straight no
pi dog	hired ruffian | revenge	needs milk for muscles
holy cow	milk please	a study of our food chain
field of grass	come get it | mud gratis	wanted a machine

then then the then the crow then the crow goes then the crow goes to then the crow goes to the

ironsmith to borrow his sickle and the ironsmith being a lonely man whose wife left him said I'll make you the finest sickle sit down in the corner where it's not so clean while I forge | the ironsmith punched bent upsetting metal on bricks and anvil | here it is my hot masterpiece but please don't carry it in your unclean beak and the crow thinks about changing his diet or bribing his ornithologist to erase the hierarchy of caste | the image of picking at and culling sparrow ribcage the taste of liver with half-formed carbohydrates overwhelms him and he says oh just place it on my wings the mynah preened them yesterday – then it becomes that story regurgitated of wings catching fire only on this side no one died dreaming of flying or fleeing

KAAK

given that our first words are always relations but tell me why
the song insisted that they be the sisters of our mother or our
father | under the bamboo bush cars keep going and experts
say that melancholia travels at the speed of object vibrations

perhaps that is why twelve crows brood on the insomniac neem
the song sings to them other names | slumberers | tale-tellers | chanters
rattlers | the betel leaf eaters | they will accept rice offerings but barter
areca nuts for lime spread on fables | the length depending on the
number or the state of their teeth | the elder the better | summoned
from a bamboo hush they have been sitting on eyelids since cicadas

colonised the base of some wheel to cry out louder in case of danger
auspices | calendar | everything is circular | lunar | diminishing or
adding up to nothing | the song no longer insists | says — let them be
no profit or remembrance are set aside for those who deal in repeating

CHEEL

opposite the tube-well was our staple land
marked to direct strangers to the old house
with red floors and black corners | standing

on the water tank brother you recited the whole area
while I watched the wind make curtains and curtains
make gridlines | at three o'clock the rooftop sizzled

then absorbed what water was left at the bottom
of the bucket | inside our kingdom resounded | solemn
with tamarinds – nothing left of it | only moss now

and mostly kites left these days to reign the upper
layers of atmosphere | kites with their shrapnel
call | obliterating | claws soaring higher and higher

till they are caught in other aerial incitements
strings sharpened with glass spinning in spools
in hands of other boys who too refuse to sleep

where do we view this from | above or below or suspended
among branches | fingers itching while we watch them rise
then fall these afternoon creatures of dust

there was nothing and there was nobody outside the window I mean but I was so scared that mother had to count my pulse to say that I was okay she laughed and said your heart is a sparrow was it you who caused that palpitation was it you outside with your scare the sister tricks I wonder now but do you remember that it happened once it almost happens all the time you and I who have seen the inside

out of the same nests
same birds eggs although
from we are yet to know
so full with stories that
and when I point out
different shapes you
silence just you and I the

and have swallowed the
where the twigs came
(sometimes the room is
the people cannot get out
that the branches are all of
smile) but when we sit in
same word comes out of

our different mouths at the same time twin birds in sudden flight was it the simultaneous fear of darkness that stirred them into a single motion? it is so astonishing that we don't want to ruin this miracle wherewhen so we sit still and watch the air turn into water and the birds into fishes and we try to extend the next moments until we hook that one word we both will say out loud next

BABUI

the weaverbird knows your great-grandmother
whose name is another word for the river who only
confides in dreams | the dream of the first to die comes

to the last to be born so the confrontation everyone wants
to hear is between two ageing mirrors in which one says you
are the worry | you want to ask the weaverbird how he keeps

the glow worms alive | some say that the dead know everything
that will happen to those not dead yet | even things other than
dying | some say the weaverbird started this rumour | you want

to ask but the weaverbird will not teach you his soft-mouthed craft
the weaverbird only says what the dead do not know or cannot tell
is if you want to know it all | sometimes as you write them down

like dreams these things happen | deaths more than births because births
take more time or are supple enough to pass | deaths more than birds
waiting for the lift | truth is when I first dreamt of the dead I did not

mind her telling me but I told her to let the others be | keep them away
from the branch within reach and she smiled | a little bird a little
death does no one harm she said the weaverbird knows

the bird saved the farmer boy the old witty way
the farmer boy saved the bird the old witty way
the wit saved the bird — here each memory falters
the premise is the same old as the oldest of all
nights with a desire to hear or maybe a desire to
tell or to be told a story that never ends if not then
a command a threat that old *or else* —

so here is a farmer boy faced with death here is
a king or the face of death or here is death with
a face of a king impatient to hear just one story
or here is a king patient to hear a story that never ends *or else* — one fine morning one fine hunter caught in his fine fine net all the birds of the
world in his net all the birds were a lot of weight
on his shoulder so he had stop to take rest it was
then that the weaverbird who knew the art of
unweaving made a soft-mouthed rupture in the
net and through this the first weaverbird escaped
into darkness into night when the king closed his
eyes a story so long it went on into the next night
when the second weaverbird escaped then
the third bird escaped the fourth one then
followed by the fifth and the sixth bird and then
the seventh weaverbird — the king said but then
how many weaverbirds were there to begin —
when the farmer boy reminded him the net had
trapped all the birds of the world the king nodded
then nodded off so until now seven weaverbirds
have escaped from the net from the story then another night was done *or else* —

the next nights after the nights of the weaverbird a different bird escaped someone smaller like a sparrow or not a sparrow it was dark so it was difficult to tell the difference in beak in feather in flight and all this while the hunter having caught all the birds of the world in his net fell into a deep sleep while from him from his net from the king the farmer boy escaped on different wings what remained in the net now was all the birds of the world minus those who escaped and then this night was dawn *or else* –

you ask me – and then?

and then I was named after your sister
and you were named after my brother

HARICHACHA

the crows are angry the treepies are here the treepies take off from the telephone wire

but the telephone wire still sways under their missing weight the treepies take no care

the crows look out for a spot to form their line but the night-blooming jasmine is full

the treepies take no care they are here they hunt for hunger they are here they screech

until their bobbing bodies make the neem tree shiver the round neem fruits shrivel

but the treepies are not worried about telephone wires they are not coin thieves either

just cinnamon bodies with throats made of bark just the loudest impossibility to speak

over the crows are angry some other birds now fly now settle in on the line with red

eyes tails so long that just for a moment the crows forget that the treepies are here

but they are here without a care and our crows cannot comprehend those other birds

who wish not to be seen but their tails are too extravagant hiding is difficult the crows

mistake these tails for a line stretched out to trip them over a wire or a lie at a stretch the first thing I broke was a bird made of coloured glass a red and green bird made green and red with glass that my mother had found at some fair she went to some years ago some years before I was born and I broke the bird and after breaking it I cried although what really happened was slightly different I was only holding the

glass bird up against	light to see through it
to see if it had a brain	a heart all those things
that I was told I had	or if it was completely
hollow but then – the	glass slipped out of
my hand and the	bird slipped out of the
glass slipped out of the	glass that held its shape
the shape of the glass	that held it in place and
instead of rising it	fell so I picked up the

broken pieces without cutting my fingers I took the broken glass bird now a broken bird now glass shards once a bird although later I refused to pick up a different bird that needed picking up but was not made of glass I held the pieces out to my mother frightened that there was nothing not a thing I could do to make the glass bird again

BOK

the crane had a habit of giving out advice | when he had no
listeners he would target widows clad in white at the river bank
on one leg contemplating fishes | the crane said that to outwit
a bear hungry for you the only way to escape was inside a gourd –
you had to carve out a human-shaped hollow and roll to safety inside it
but to outwit a tiger a goat had only to rely on an echo and speak without
bleating | to outwit a king and steal coins from his treasury a bird like
the tailorbird had to find the epiglottis and make sure the king was ticklish
if the trick was successful the king would even have his nose | chopped off
by accident by bird's design but for a foolproof conspiracy against the rice
stealing thief there were no better compatriots than the wood-apple | the catfish
a barber's blade and some cow dung | the crane went on making impossible
tales to keep himself engaged | the stories when good lured out fishes from
their depths | the old women who watched his art grow whispered to each other
someday he will inspire the greatest or the longest tale but perhaps he will be
so much in love with himself or another he would have to give up his life

SHOKUN

meanwhile – in a place not far from – in another time –
they overfed the bull to turn him into cash cow
goutless pure calcium | he turned into a super plougher
he lived on and even learnt to love the yoke

in a place far far away – meanwhile – in our time –
the Indian vulture loved only cattle flesh more
than gambling | when the time came he got what he wanted
but lost his race to the poisoned bull who spoke in wheels

meanwhile – in a place not far from – in older days –
the vulture in his full plumage had the capacity to chase
chariots | see through disguises | he was hired by husbands
suspicious of their wives | but there too a sacrifice | euthanasia

unwarranted intervention on high streets | meanwhile – even
when the forester drew a circle the vulture could not overcome
his habit of transboundary feeding | meanwhile – these days –
in a place not far from – in these suspicious times – he prays

to the forester whose friend the scientist regulates
an incubator round as an egg | gambles with the right amount
of heat | asks him | tell me as it happened right from the start

you ask me – and then?

    then nothing

                                                                         you ask me – why?
                                                                         you ask me – how?

              I would have to tell you everything
              that happened in order for you to see
              what did not happen and that itself
              is nothing but a true impossibility

                                                                   you ask me – and then?

              then, nothing – what if I really have nothing
              to tell? why won't you believe me? why
              won't you believe what I have to say?

                              you mock me – why won't I believe you?
                            I know you – I know that when there's nothing
                                            left – it's then that you invent

these names did not stay – her first when she was named after the call of a peacock
her sister after the sound of a *koel* her sister after the way birds alight on branches
I was named to rhyme with my brother's name – my brother was just named
just two times before my birth – then I was named
after your sister and you were named after my brother

GUBGUBI PAKHI

this name is probably a lie –
because I cannot track this one down to Its commoner name | I cannot find | Its feeding habits | Its wingspan | if It is migratory | yet It exists It is real the name may be made up | what name is not made up | the guttural in the grass – real | the red eyes staring one at a time – real one at a time | the big black feather It once left behind – real although lost | real as in my memory but some others will be able to vouch for Its reality | you may verify | here is my definition of It –

if I did not eat my lunch – It would come get me
if I did not sleep – It would come get me
if I did not wake up in time – It would come get me
if I did not finish my lines – It has already placed Its beak upon my pencil

you might as well give It another name | since we have shed our old names we might as well call It the *if-I-did-not-pakhi* or the *be-a-good-little-girl-or-else-pakhi* or something else something that chimes when uttered | the name of a song for instance the name of the arrangement of notes in a particular song sung at a particular time of the day for instance | dawn for instance | now it does not come outside my window anymore | I do not eat my lunch I pretend I do not sleep I do not wake up in time and I refuse to finish my lines for I want to know I want to know how It would

MURGI

this is how the story ends – with the old woman lying
down | true I have wrung my word bank dry but why
must the little plant wither her head so | the little plant
shudders | true I wither at the end of your words but how
dare the cow threaten to eat me | the cow kicks a hoof full
of dust on the twilight road | how dare the farmer boy
still not take me home | the farmer boy skips a stone
on grass | it sinks it knows that he has not eaten all day
someone at the farmer boy's home says | how dare
that banana tree deprive us of plates and humiliated
the banana tree weeps | if only it would rain | eavesdropping
this the frogs agree | we would summon clouds had our tribe
increased | how dare the snake gobble us whole – at this
the krait slinks back to fill his stomach | why ever shall I not eat

the room is full with people   you and I are meant to know
everyone in the room has a   story to tell and they wait for
us to finish our mind games   but we have only just begun
(their stories cannot be new   anyway) they start with tales
of loss of theft where some   one leaves or is left behind I
admire the trees outside this   afternoon cannot tell what
you are thinking it is not as   easy anymore I think every
thing changed when you left   the room is full with people
you and I are meant to meet   someone calls out our names
to say the usual   how much   you've both changed we do
not know this person and I   do not understand why the

curtain is moving in a strange   way but your eyes are fixed
on the stranger who seems to   know us and our stories well
is there someone outside the   window something lurking is
this room secure with stories   dying to be told? you see my
fear and investigate we are all   okay it is only a bird a little
sparrow caught here trying to   get in do you mean get out I
ask so you confess it was me   when you were three   it was
me outside trying to scare you   I had tapped on the glass but
look now this little sparrow is   trapped no more but I hear a
heart pounding or is that the   sound of stories being told I
ask you and you say it's okay   it is nothing there is nobody

you are the worry between love and what you have not said yet

when I was four and staring at pictures of words I thought were animals or numbers I thought were birds you were seven fast swallowing facts | you had eight books of facts that I never touched but perhaps if I did I would have known better than to feed balls of dough to our fishes perhaps if I did I would have known the following myths –

all tiny animals can be kept alive with milk and bread | fishes floating in water means they are happy on a holiday | your closed fist is roughly the size of your heart rib-caged | mother bird will abandon baby bird if touched by human hands | milk and bread invite the dead into houses

fact – because I did not know I abandoned the nestling | or fact – because I was afraid of touching of trembling not of its consequence | but that same year you told me that there was too much sorrow in the world that my tears could never be enough for all the sorrows that I would see fact – what a lot of weight off my shoulders | myth – you thought you could stop caring altogether

but you taught me how to read well | by how I mean what | by read I mean live

PYANCHA

I give you an owl
her feathers | beak | pupils
are porcelain | everything
is white | I give you a blind

owl the size of a closed fist

you know as I do that in the first
story it is owl and monkey
the exile siblings who float from
sea to sea until they find some
of life's right things | I know you

have forgotten some details
the bug in the blood box |
the safe clamour of faces
asleep behind glass | I give

you an owl to remind you

of that first story and what
happened to us afterwards –
the places we went | the floors
we kissed | the secrets we thrust
under the foundation sand where
our house stands now where we
have not stood for a while | not
with those dreams intact anyway

this owl is an insomniac

let her repeat to you her blind
tales | leave her by the window
wherever you are | let her
reflect and bring closer some
of the oldest and wildest stars

when a bird   ing not to be
when a bird   selfish when
enters a room   a room opens
the window   opens up to
bbbdiesbbb   rrrrbirdsrrrr
a glassy death   says death is

when a glass   a bird trying
when a glass   not to be sel-
enters a bird   fish or trying
the window   not to be glass
iiiisaysiiiii   dddwhenddd
was only try-   a bird enters

NOTES

The Bengali words and phrases in the poem 'Why Did You Stop Writing' are copied directly from my father's 1979 notebook. 'Eucalyptus, You' and 'Poster' are the two poem titles mentioned in the Bengali script. 'Dear poet, how very difficult' is a rough translation of the words that 'something happens to'. In the same notebook, I found many versions of the line 'King of the kingdom of nothing am I, to the left of the chest lies a stitched heart, weighing three hundred and forty grams'. The long title of the poem about the Farraka Barrage may be translated (in a supremely awkward way) as 'Thinking of numerous things while watching the moon on the twelfth day of the lunar fortnight'. The first of the last two questions may be translated as 'How will we smell each other?' and the second one as 'Dear poet, who says there is no meaning to staying alive?'.

The 'Future Library' poems were triggered by Katie Paterson's astonishing public art project (of the same name; 'Framitidsbiblioteket', in the Norwegian), which involves tending to 1000 spruce trees that were planted in 2014, somewhere outside Oslo, to create and curate a library for the future. For the next 100 years, one writer will be contributing a text to the library every year, and these unread manuscripts will be held in secrecy, until the year 2114, when they will be printed with paper supplied by the spruce forest. Flagged off by Margaret Atwood handing over her text 'Scribbler Moon', Paterson's art work is an experiment to see if text produced in the present will find receptive readers in the unknown future. In the 'Future Library' poems, there is also an acknowledgement of Mark Fisher's nod to Franco Berardi's 'cancellation of the future' in Fisher's book *Ghosts of My Life*.

The poem 'Salt' was written for an Emma Press anthology celebrating urban interpretations of the Ovidian metamorphoses myths; the poem was written after being haunted by *The Vegetarian* by Han Kang, translated from the Korean by Deborah Smith.

The question in the final line of 'Hazardous' is the first of the thirty-six questions that psychologists Arthur Aron et al. listed in their 1997 study to see if intimacy between strangers could be accelerated in an experimental context. In 2015, the 'closeness-generating' questionnaire reappeared in the popular news cycle after the publication of a *New York Times* 'Modern Love' essay by Mandy Len Catron.

'Dinosaur on Wheels' tucks in a line (in italics) from Lyn Hejinian's *My Life*.

'What I Can't Distil' has been written after 'What's Broken' by Dorianne Laux.

There are two sly winks at Philip Larkin in 'By a Different Line'.

I want to acknowledge my newfound sisterhood with the works of Jane Wong in the poem 'Your Succulents Need a Drought'.

'And Other Stories': Some of the content in this series of poems has been inspired by two Bangla children's classics, recounting animal folklore and fairy tales: *Tuntunir Boi* (1910) by Upendrakishore Ray Chowdhury and *Thakumar Jhuli* (1907) compiled by Dakshinaranjan Mitra Majumdar. The tailorbird (tuntuni) is the protagonist of many of the stories in *Tuntunir Boi* (*The Tailorbird's Book*) in which he outwits cats, tigers and kings. A few of these plots are referred to in the poem 'Bok'. The poem 'Chorui' is a retelling of the story 'Chorai Aar Kaaker Katha'. There is a reference to the Bengali lullaby 'Ghum Parani Mashi Pishi' (anonymous) in the poem 'Kaak'. I may have unwittingly combined two or three folk tales involving hunters and birds while retelling the never-ending story in 'The Bird Saved'. Some references to the fairy tales compiled in *Thakumar Jhuli* (*Grandmother's Sack of Stories*) are made in the poem 'Pyancha'. 'Murgi' is the retelling of the verse envoi that playfully concludes the same collection, in which, accused of not having more stories to tell, the old woman passes on the blame to the wilting plant (*Amaranthus viridis*), who then passes it on to the grazing cow and so on, until the blame game reaches the snake. The poem titles in the series are common names for birds in the Bengali. However, 'Gubgubi Pakhi' is a questionable species, which I have not been able to trace and perhaps is something my mother dreamed up.

ACKNOWLEDGEMENTS

Sincere gratitude to all the editors and publishers of the following anthologies and journals where some of the poems in this collection appeared in early versions: 'Poraghati' – *My Lot is the Sky: An Anthology of Poems by Asian Women* Eds. Melissa Powers & Rena Minegishi (Singapore: Math Paper Press, 2018); 'Salt' – *Urban Myths and Legends* Eds. Emma Wright & Rachel Piercey (Birmingham: The Emma Press, 2016); *40 under 40: An Anthology of Post Globalisation Poetry* Eds. Nabina Das & Semeen Ali (Mumbai: Poetrywala, 2016); 'Setting', 'the stains on the tablecloth are trying to say something' – *UEA MA Poetry 2015 Anthology* (Norwich: Eggbox Publishing, 2015); 'babui' – *Oxford Poetry Magazine* 'Crossings' Issue; 'chorui' – *The Suburban Review* Volume 7: Writers of Colour; 'lightning never strikes in straight lines' – *Helter Skelter New Writing Vol 4* Eds. Janice Pariat, Jerry Pinto & Nitoo Das; 'dim light' – *I am part of that generation: PBS Student Poetry Competition Anthology 2014* selected by Jane Yeh; 'Mnemonic' – *The Unsettled Winter: The RLP Award Anthology 2013*; 'they have more to say' – *And Other Poems*; 'other small disasters' – *The Missing Slate*, 'I Dream in Inglish' feature curated by the Great India Poetry Collective; 'possibly octagonal' – TFQM, 'there was nothing' – Café Writers, poem of the month July 2015; 'Plot' – the Ofi Press/YPN collaboration; 'Coventry' – *The Scribbler*; 'Pickling' – *Jaggery*, Volume 1.

★

How this language, not wholly mine, became the language with which I navigate the world is, of course, a long story. Some of the enchantment happened very early on, through illustrated books and at school. Always grateful to my teachers there. Grateful especially to Goutam Bhattacharya, for handing a sheaf of Szymborska's mortal hand revenge to a seventeen-year-old me one evening in that bizarre room in Barrackpore. Everyone at St Stephen's College for continuing/critiquing the enchantment, especially N.P. Ashley and Anannya Dasgupta. And Ashish Roy, for unexpected advice on sharpness of lines, and a coffee that will be forever pending. Nitoo Das, for early encouragement and first workshop. Kaushik Chaudhuri, for pushing me off the nest, three times and counting. In England, I was privileged to discuss some of these poems with David Morley, Sophie Robinson, and Tiffany Atkinson – that afternoon we spread out the bird poems on your office floor, something shifted in my brain. Avrina, Bee, Billy, Daryl, Eleanor, Elizabeth, Mo, Tom, fellow workshop companions, lucky to have met you all. Thank you, Juliana Spahr, for changing the way I looked at the lyric in forty minutes. Anjum Hasan, for the kind words. Vahni Capildeo, thank you. Emptying out shelves full of gratitude to libraries and their keepers. And what about the internet as a point of strange confluence? Readers, who have dropped unexpected notes. Editors of literary journals. Translators, for lifting veils off so much magic. I have been fortunate to receive support from various organizations running writing prizes, so thank you: Annie Chandy, of the erstwhile Unisun publications; Linda Ashok, who runs the Raedleaf prize; Sarita and Anmol Vellani, who support so many young Indian artists through Toto Funds the Arts. Thanks also to the Malcolm Bradbury foundation at the University of East Anglia, for the generous grant. Todd Swift and Edwin Smet at Eyewear Publishing. Cate Myddleton-Evans, thank you for the generous attention to the manuscript. Alice, for quiet times. Avinab, for conjuring a fox. Chloe, for postcards and pasta. Michael, for pointing out bird houses and other details by the Wensum. Prerna, for beverage and bats. Rahul, for questioning the crane. Serena, for all that you do. Zoe, for mad collaborations. Maybe none of this would have happened if I had not stayed on in Delhi in 2010. For making this home: Subhalakshmi, Sayan, Saumya, Radhika, Ahona. And Urvashi, for sitting on the balcony ledge with a fat book of poems and reading my mind.

Pagol and clan, for perpetuating the silly.

And, my family. Without you, nothing.

EYEWEAR PUBLISHING

TITLES INCLUDE

EYEWEAR POETRY

ELSPETH SMITH DANGEROUS CAKES
CALEB KLACES BOTTLED AIR
GEORGE ELLIOTT CLARKE ILLICIT SONNETS
HANS VAN DE WAARSENBURG THE PAST IS NEVER DEAD
BARBARA MARSH TO THE BONEYARD
DON SHARE UNION
SHEILA HILLIER HOTEL MOONMILK
SJ FOWLER THE ROTTWEILER'S GUIDE TO THE DOG OWNER
JEMMA BORG THE ILLUMINATED WORLD
KEIRAN GODDARD FOR THE CHORUS
COLETTE SENSIER SKINLESS
ANDREW SHIELDS THOMAS HARDY LISTENS TO LOUIS ARMSTRONG
JAN OWEN THE OFFHAND ANGEL
A.K. BLAKEMORE HUMBERT SUMMER
SEAN SINGER HONEY & SMOKE
HESTER KNIBBE HUNGERPOTS
MEL PRYOR SMALL NUCLEAR FAMILY
ELSPETH SMITH KEEPING BUSY
TONY CHAN FOUR POINTS FOURTEEN LINES
MARIA APICHELLA PSALMODY
ALICE ANDERSON THE WATERMARK
BEN PARKER THE AMAZING LOST MAN
REBECCA GAYLE HOWELL AMERICAN PURGATORY
MARION MCCREADY MADAME ECOSSE
MARIELA GRIFFOR DECLASSIFIED
MARK YAKICH THE DANGEROUS BOOK OF POETRY FOR PLANES
HASSAN MELEHY A MODEST APOCALYPSE
KATE NOAKES PARIS, STAGE LEFT
U.S. DHUGA THE SIGHT OF A GOOSE GOING BAREFOOT
TERENCE TILLER THE COLLECTED POEMS
MATTHEW STEWART THE KNIVES OF VILLALEJO
PAUL MULDOON SADIE AND THE SADISTS
JENNA CLAKE FORTUNE COOKIE
TARA SKURTU THE AMOEBA GAME
MANDY KAHN GLENN GOULD'S CHAIR
CAL FREEMAN FIGHT SONGS
TIM DOOLEY WEEMOED
MATTHEW PAUL THE EVENING ENTERTAINMENT
NIALL BOURKE DID YOU PUT THE WEASELS OUT?
USHA KISHORE IMMIGRANT
DUSTIN PEARSON MILLENIAL ROOST
LEAH UMANSKY THE BARBAROUS CENTURY
STEVE KRONEN HOMAGE TO MISTRESS OPPENHEIMER
FAISAL MOHYUDDIN THE DISPLACED CHILDREN OF DISPLACED CHILDREN
ALEX HOUEN RING CYCLE
COLIN DARDIS THE X OF Y
JAMES FINNEGAN HALF-OPEN DOOR
RICKY RAY FEALTY
SOHINI BASAK WE LIVE IN THE NEWNESS OF SMALL DIFFERENCES